ANCIENT
MESOPOTAMIA
INSIDE OUT

Ellen Rodger

Crabtree Publishing Company
www.crabtreebooks.com

Author: Ellen Rodger

Editors: Sarah Eason, Kelly Spence, Janine Deschenes, and Kathy Middleton

Editorial director: Kathy Middleton

Design: Paul Myerscough

Cover design: Paul Myerscough

Photo research: Rachel Blount

Proofreader: Wendy Scavuzzo

Production coordinator and Prepress technician: Tammy McGarr

Print coordinator: Margaret Amy Salter

Consultant: John Malam, archaeologist

Written and produced for Crabtree Publishing Company by Calcium Creative

Front Cover
BKGD: A reconstruction of the Ishtar Gate, the eighth gate of the city of Babylon. The original was one of the Seven Wonders of the Ancient World.
Inset: From the Mesopotamian era, the Ram in a Thicket is made from gold, copper, shell, limestone, and lapis lazuli.
Title Page
BKGD: The Ziggurat of Ur, a Sumerian temple built during the Early Bronze Age. A ziggurat is a pyramid with steps and levels, often made of sun-baked mud bricks.
Inset: The Statue of Ebih-Il, from an ancient city in Syria. The statue of a praying figure is made of gypsum, schist, shells, and lapis lazuli.

Photo Credits:

t=Top, bl=Bottom Left, br=Bottom Right

Alamy: World History Archive: p. 9t; Getty Images: Werner Forman: p. 15b;

LACMA www.lacma.org: The Phil Berg Collection: p. 21b; Gift of Robert Blaugrund: p. 29t;

Shutterstock: Borna Mirahmadian: p. 22–23; ChameleonsEye: p. 26–27; Homo Cosmicos: p. 1bg, p. 18–19, p. 28b; Robert Jakatics: p. 13b; Kamira: p. 17t; Nexus 7: p. 8–9; Radiokafka: p. 24–25; Rasoulali: p. 6–7, p. 10–11, p. 12–13; SJ Travel Photo and Video: p. 4–5; IR Stone: p. 3, p. 6–17, p. 20–21;

Wikimedia Commons: Osama Shukir Muhammed Amin FRCP(Glasg): p. 23b; Mbzt: p. 11b; 1934-1935: excavated by André Parrot. Place: Temple of Ishtar at Mari: p. 1fg, p. 25b; Prioryman: p. 27t; Bjørn Christian Tørrissen: p. 14–15; Whiteghost. ink: p. 28–29.

Map p. 5 by Geoff Ward. Artwork p. 29 by Venetia Dean.

Cover: Shutterstock: Rasoulali (bg); Wikimedia Commons: British Museum (br).

Library and Archives Canada Cataloguing in Publication

Rodger, Ellen, author
    Ancient Mesopotamia inside out / Ellen Rodger.

(Ancient worlds inside out)
Includes index.
Issued in print and electronic formats.
ISBN 978-0-7787-2880-1 (hardcover).--
ISBN 978-0-7787-2894-8 (softcover).--
ISBN 978-1-4271-1849-3 (HTML)

    1. Iraq--Civilization--To 634--Juvenile literature.
2. Iraq--Antiquities--Juvenile literature. 3. Material culture--Iraq--Juvenile literature. 4. Iraq--History--To 634--Juvenile literature. I. Title.

DS69.5.R64 2017   j935   C2016-907263-0
                                   C2016-907264-9

Library of Congress Cataloging-in-Publication Data

Names: Rodger, Ellen, author.
Title: Ancient Mesopotamia inside out / Ellen Rodger.
Description: New York, New York : Crabtree Publishing Company, [2017] | Series: Ancient worlds inside out | Includes index.
Identifiers: LCCN 2016058590 (print) | LCCN 2017003326 (ebook) | ISBN 9780778728801 (reinforced library binding : alkaline paper) | ISBN 9780778728948 (paperback : alkaline paper) | ISBN 9781427118493 (Electronic HTML)
Subjects: LCSH: Iraq--Civilization--To 634--Juvenile literature. | Iraq--Antiquities--Juvenile literature.
Classification: LCC DS71 .R65 2017 (print) | LCC DS71 (ebook) | DDC 935--dc23
LC record available at https://lccn.loc.gov/2016058590

Crabtree Publishing Company

www.crabtreebooks.com   1-800-387-7650

Printed in Canada/032017/EF20170202

Published in Canada
Crabtree Publishing
616 Welland Ave.
St. Catharines, Ontario
L2M 5V6

Published in the United States
Crabtree Publishing
PMB 59051
350 Fifth Avenue, 59th Floor
New York, New York 10118

Published in the United Kingdom
Crabtree Publishing
Maritime House
Basin Road North, Hove
BN41 1WR

Published in Australia
Crabtree Publishing
3 Charles Street
Coburg North
VIC, 3058

CONTENTS

WHO WERE THE ANCIENT MESOPOTAMIANS?

The region called Mesopotamia has been home to four major civilizations, many cultures, and several empires stretching over 6,000 years. Because of this, it has been called the "cradle of civilization."

Land Between Two Rivers

Mesopotamia's name comes from the ancient Greek words for "between two rivers." Mesopotamia was made up of the **city-states** that grew between and around the Tigris River and Euphrates River. The remains of Mesopotamia are located in what are now Iraq, Kuwait, parts of Syria, southern Turkey, and western Iran. More than 6,000 years ago, the Sumerians—Mesopotamia's first known civilization— began farming and building cities in southern Iraq. They developed the first written language, and they are also said to have invented the wheel, arithmetic, war chariots, the first written system of laws, and **agricultural irrigation**.

Way, Way Back

The Sumerians were not the only people to live in Mesopotamia. Many groups of people settled there over thousands of years. The earliest recorded people in Mesopotamia began living there and banding together in small villages from 4000–5500 B.C.E. They were called the Ubaidians, named after the village site of Tell al-Ubaid, where evidence of their **habitation** was found. Much is still unknown about them, but **archaeologists** describe them as farmers and animal herders. Each group of people who lived in Mesopotamia added to, and built upon, the achievements of the previous group.

What Is an Ancient Civilization?

Large settlements of people formed the basis of the first civilizations. Through practices such as farming and the development of writing systems, government, and class systems, the settlements of people grew into large cities. These ancient civilizations led to the later development of present-day cities, states, and countries.

The Euphrates River is 1,740 miles (2,800 km) long. It is the longest river in western Asia, which reaches from Turkey to Yemen and Oman in the south.

Key

- The ancient lands of Mesopotamia
- Present-day borders

This map shows the ancient cities of Mesopotamia, situated close to the Tigris and Euphrates rivers.

Turkey

Syria

Iran

ASSYRIA

Nineveh

Nimrud

Tigris River

Euphrates River

AKKAD

Iraq

Babylon

BABYLONIA

Lagash

Uruk

SUMER

Jordan

Ur

Eridu

Kuwait

Persian Gulf

Saudi Arabia

DIGGING UP THE PAST

In 1872, **historian** George Smith translated the words written on a clay tablet found in the ruins of the ancient Mesopotamian city of Nineveh. The words were written in cuneiform, the system of writing developed by the ancient Sumerians. It contained a story of a ship, a dove, a flood, and a man who wanted to save the world. Smith's discovery of the myth triggered a frenzy of interest in the civilizations of Mesopotamia. It led to more research, **excavations**, and new discoveries.

Rediscovering the Ancient World

In the years since Smith's translation, many more cuneiform tablets have been translated. They show that Mesopotamian civilizations had **sophisticated** cultures and developed ways of writing to record their stories. Their writings have been valuable in showing us what life was like in Mesopotamia thousands of years ago. We can also learn about Mesopotamia from physical remains, such as pottery and ancient **temples**, or places of worship.

Under the Ground

Many **artifacts** are found buried under the ground over time. The archaeologists who study **prehistoric** and ancient cultures are like detectives. They use many techniques and tools. They survey sites where they believe ancient peoples lived. They dig up these sites, and use science to help them determine the age of objects.

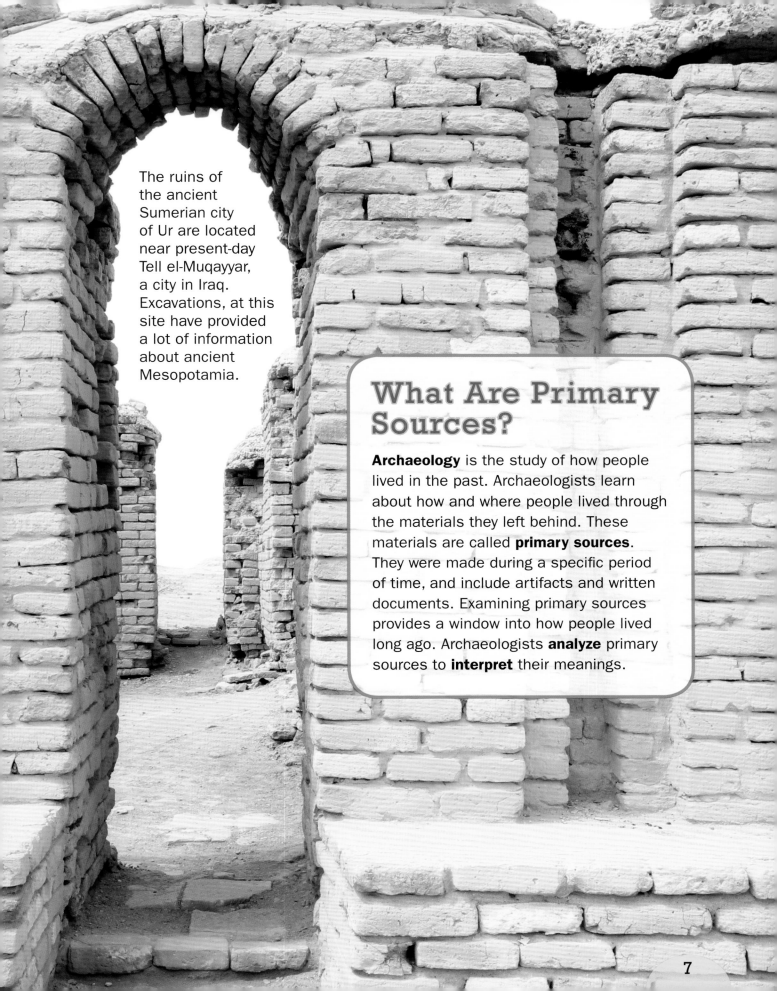

The ruins of the ancient Sumerian city of Ur are located near present-day Tell el-Muqayyar, a city in Iraq. Excavations, at this site have provided a lot of information about ancient Mesopotamia.

What Are Primary Sources?

Archaeology is the study of how people lived in the past. Archaeologists learn about how and where people lived through the materials they left behind. These materials are called **primary sources**. They were made during a specific period of time, and include artifacts and written documents. Examining primary sources provides a window into how people lived long ago. Archaeologists **analyze** primary sources to **interpret** their meanings.

BETWEEN TWO RIVERS

Thousands of years ago, the lands of Mesopotamia were home to plant life, and the people who lived there were able to grow crops. This is because the Tigris and Euphrates flooded twice a year. However, over time, the rivers changed direction as they flowed across their floodplain, leaving the ruins of Mesopotamia to sit in the midst of very dry desert.

Flooding and Farming

The Tigris and Euphrates, and their smaller rivers and streams flowing in and around them, make up a river system that flows south through Mesopotamia. Their flooding brought **silt** from the mountains into the lower hills and plains. The silt helped make the soil good for growing crops. Early Mesopotamian cultures took wild plants and combined them to produce stronger crops. For example, they combined emmer wheat with goat grass to make a plant that could produce more food. Stable food sources helped nearby villages grow into city-states. The city-state of Uruk was home to 50,000 people at its **peak**, or highest population.

Southern Marshes

In the south, a region of **marshes**, or wetlands, **lagoons**, and small lakes covered thousands of miles of territory. The marshes were rich in wetland wildlife, including birds, snakes, and otters. The people who lived in these marshes farmed, fished, and raised livestock. They used the tall marsh reeds to make homes and boats.

The Euphrates River continues to be a vital, life-giving source of water for people living along its course today.

Babylonian map of the world

oversea lands

neighboring
city-states

Babylon

sea

Euphrates
River

History Up Close

Babylon was a major city on the Euphrates. This map, carved into a clay tablet, offers a peek at how the Babylonians understood the world. It dates from 700 B.C.E., and was found in Sippar in Iraq. In the inner circle, Babylon is marked as a rectangle (above the hole in the middle). Two lines in the center represent the Euphrates. The area is surrounded by a circle representing a salty ocean. Beyond the sea are lands marked as triangles. Closer to Babylon are neighboring city-states, marked as small circles. The idea was to show Babylon's position in the world, in relation to other places.

RULERS AND KINGS

At different times, Mesopotamia was home to several different civilizations, kingdoms, and empires. Within the civilizations, there were city-states. From time to time, one city-state tried to conquer another.

Thousands of Years of Government

Sumer (3500–2300 B.C.E.) was the first Mesopotamian civilization, and it included the city-states of Uruk, Kish, Ur, and Nippur. The Akkadian Empire (2300–2000 B.C.E.) was centered in the city of Akkad. The Babylonian Empire (2000–1100 B.C.E.) emerged in the plains south of what is now Baghdad, Iraq. The Assyrian Empire (612–599 B.C.E.) developed along the Tigris River in upper Mesopotamia.

Kings and More Kings

In ancient Mesopotamia, most regions were ruled by kings. One of the greatest kings of ancient Mesopotamia was Sargon the Great. He ruled Akkadia from 2334–2279 B.C.E. The title was hereditary and so, passed from a father to his eldest son. Because titles were passed down, dynasties arose in which one family ruled for many years. The kings were supposed to care for their people and ensure that their kingdoms survived. They did this by making their people pay **taxes** and provide free **labor**, or work. Some people were required to serve in the military, while others tended crops or built **canals**, or human-made rivers.

The ruins of the ancient city of Babylon are located 59 miles (94 km) southwest of the city of Baghdad in Iraq. Some parts of Babylon have been reconstructed.

Hammurabi, king of Babylon, is probably the world's most famous early lawmaker. The Law Code of Hammurabi, a list of 282 laws and punishments, dates back to 1754 B.C.E. Found on clay tablets and stone **stelae**, the code includes laws that allow divorce, punish theft, and control **trade**. Law 196 is one of the most well-known laws. It says that punishment should be "an eye for an eye, a tooth for a tooth." Hammurabi's laws are carved into this stone stela that dates from 1792–1750 B.C.E. This stela was discovered at the city of Sippar, where it would have been on display.

Law Code of Hammurabi

Dig Deeper!

Why do you think written laws helped a civilization develop?

DAILY LIFE

Archaeologists look at **tells**, tombs, and the cities themselves to find out about daily life in Mesopotamia. Tells are hills or mounds of earth that were once the site of ancient settlements. They show archaeologists what materials people used for building, what foods they ate, and what jobs they did. Tombs also reveal many things, including a person's wealth and status during their life.

Treasure from Ur

The ruins of the city of Ur in southern Iraq have provided archaeologists with a lot of information. They show that the Mesopotamian cultures were divided into **social classes**, or groups of people based on their wealth or status. Kings and rulers were at the top. There was also a wealthy class of landowners, priests, priestesses, and government officials such as **scribes**. **Merchants**, or people who sell goods, farmers, laborers, servants, and slaves made up the other classes.

The Queen's Tomb

Queen Puabi must have been a wealthy and powerful woman in Ur, because her tomb was so extravagant. It was uncovered by archaeologist Leonard Woolley, who excavated 1,800 graves in Ur between 1922 and 1934. The tomb contained gold, musical instruments, and makeup made from colored dyes. She also had gold headdresses, jewelry, and dinnerware.

Kings to the Lower-Class Groups

Kings made sure the city-state or empire was successful. Priests and priestesses performed religious ceremonies. The people of Ur believed in many gods. Priests and priestesses made sure the gods were respected. One of the best-known priestesses was Enheduanna, **high priestess**, or main priestess, of Ur. Unlike most women, she was educated, and wrote poems to the Moon god Nanna. Scribes, merchants, and **craftspeople** helped create wealth and made trade goods. Most people belonged to the lower-class groups of farmers, brick-makers, fishermen, artists, and construction workers.

This reproduction, or copy, of the Ishtar Gate can be found in Babylon today.

History Up Close

The Ishtar Gate was the main entrance to Babylon. Built for King Nebuchadnezzar II in 575 B.C.E., its bricks were covered in tiles **glazed**, or painted and baked to a shiny coating, in a deep-blue color. After passing through the gate, the street leading to the city center was lined with tile **panels**, or raised sections, featuring lions, such as this one. These animals were symbols of Ishtar, the goddess of love and war. The lions represented protection of the street and led people to the city's temple.

lion panel

THE FERTILE CRESCENT

Mesopotamia is part of the Fertile Crescent, a crescent-shaped area of fertile land surrounded by dry desert. The earliest people gathered wild plants and hunted animals. Over time, they grew plants themselves and raised animals. Farming first developed there around 9000 B.C.E., before there were great cities. These farmers were the first to grow ancient cereal crops and use milk from cattle, sheep, and goats to make butter and cheese.

The First Farmers

The Tigris and Euphrates rivers flooded each year, leaving fertile silt behind. The large amount of fresh water allowed the Mesopotamians to **irrigate**, or water their crops. Mesopotamian farmers grew ancient wheat crops such as einkorn wheat and emmer wheat. They also grew barley, beans, peas, cabbage, carrots, lettuce, and spinach. Farmers bred livestock such as goats, sheep, geese, and ducks. They also made beer and wine. Grain was such an essential part of the food that was eaten, that workers were sometimes paid in grain.

Growing Clothing

Sheep were not just for milk and meat. Their woolly fleece was cut off and used to make clothing, blankets, and rugs. Farmers also grew a plant called flax, which had fibers that were made into linen cloth. Shoes and sandals were made from leather or reeds from the marshes. Later, the Assyrians grew cotton, and used it to make robes, skirts, and other everyday garments.

The floodplain of the Tigris River provided fertile soil that was suitable for farming.

History Up Close

Mesopotamia was the first farming region in the world. The goats raised in Mesopotamia are likely descended from the wild or Bezoar goat. Mesopotamians were also the first to use oxen to pull **ards**, or light plows. The **impression** below was made with an Akkadian cylinder seal that dates from 2340–2180 B.C.E. These seals were cylinders with figures, letters, and designs cut into them. It shows a farmer leading an ox that is pulling a plow. Two other men guide the plow. These plows scratched shallow **furrows**, or grooves, in the soil, then seeds were planted.

plow impression

ORIGINATORS AND INVENTORS

The Mesopotamians created many things we still use today, including the wheel, maps, glazed pottery, and a system of counting. Their innovations and inventions were practical and made life easier.

Wooden Wheels

The wheel, first invented around 3500 B.C.E., changed transportation forever. It allowed bulky loads, such as grain and other crops, to be carried long distances by ox cart. The first wheels were made of solid wood and rotated on **axles**. Mesopotamians also began using chariots about 2000 B.C.E. Chariots were used for hunting and in war. They could easily carry two to three people, and were very fast when pulled by horses.

Counting in Units of 60

Some records show that the Mesopotamian counting system was created as a way to record large payments or measurements in farming and trade. The sexagesimal system was a math system based on the number 60. It used symbols for specific numbers, and recorded them on cones made from clay. The number 60 was used because it can be divided evenly by many numbers, including 1, 2, 3, 4, 5, 6, 10, 12, 15, 20, and 30. We use this system today to count time, with 60 minutes in an hour, and 60 seconds in a minute. Clay tablets show that the ancient Mesopotamians also calculated the area of geometric shapes such as rectangles and triangles. These were used to measure land for farming and building.

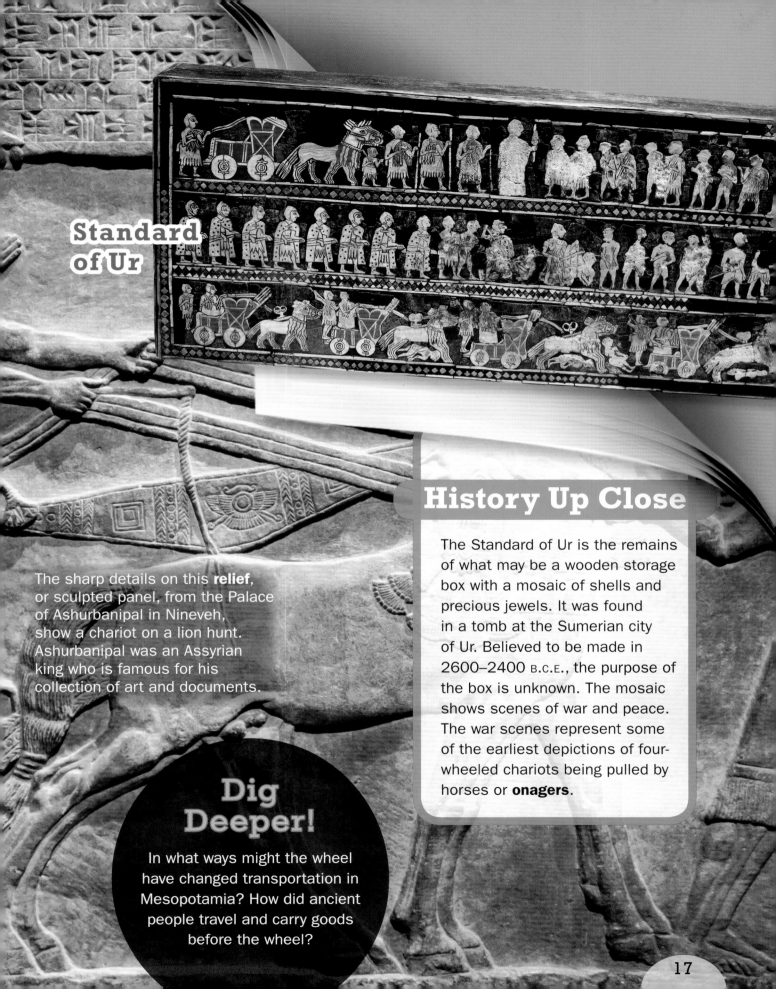

Standard of Ur

The sharp details on this **relief**, or sculpted panel, from the Palace of Ashurbanipal in Nineveh, show a chariot on a lion hunt. Ashurbanipal was an Assyrian king who is famous for his collection of art and documents.

Dig Deeper!

In what ways might the wheel have changed transportation in Mesopotamia? How did ancient people travel and carry goods before the wheel?

History Up Close

The Standard of Ur is the remains of what may be a wooden storage box with a mosaic of shells and precious jewels. It was found in a tomb at the Sumerian city of Ur. Believed to be made in 2600–2400 B.C.E., the purpose of the box is unknown. The mosaic shows scenes of war and peace. The war scenes represent some of the earliest depictions of four-wheeled chariots being pulled by horses or **onagers**.

17

FEATS OF ARCHITECTURE

Bricks were one of the most common building materials in ancient Mesopotamia. They were used to construct homes, as well as public buildings. Mud bricks were made from mud and straw, and dried in the Sun. Fired bricks were hardened at high temperatures in a **kiln**, or oven. Both types were used in the most famous examples of Mesopotamian architecture—enormous stepped platforms called ziggurats.

Leveled Structure

The Mesopotamians were skilled architects. The remains of several ziggurats show that they were built using layered platforms and **buttresses**. Ziggurats were massive structures, which were believed to be the link between heaven and earth. They had from two to seven levels, with a temple at the top. Many ziggurat temples were built outside of city walls.

Canal Builders

The Mesopotamian people built some of the earliest canals because of the seasonal flooding of the Tigris and Euphrates rivers. The canals helped the people stop the floodwater from damaging the land around it. They also helped to irrigate farmlands. In 705 B.C.E., the Assyrians built **aqueducts** to carry water from canals to where it was needed. The remains of these canals can still be seen today.

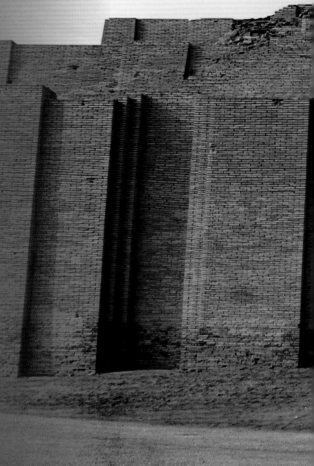

The massive Ziggurat of Ur was originally 70 to 100 feet (21 to 30 m) high. Its mud and fired bricks were much heavier than the bricks used today. The ziggurat was built around 2100 B.C.E. by King Ur-Nammu.

History Up Close

For thousands of years, this mud brick was buried in the ruins of an ancient Sumerian city in Iraq. Stamped with the name of King Ur-Nammu, it was believed to have been made for a building in the city-state of Nippur, where the king had his **coronation**. Ur-Nammu's rule dates from 2047–2030 B.C.E. He is known for having ordered the construction of many ziggurats throughout his kingdom.

stamped brick

EDUCATED SOCIETY

The Sumerians developed the first system of writing about 5,000 years ago. The earliest form of writing used pictograms, or symbols that represented ideas and words. These pictograms developed into a system called cuneiform. Cuneiform means "wedge-shaped." This wedge-shaped script was used by all the Mesopotamian civilizations for more than 3,000 years.

Recording History

Cuneiform script was used to record everything from **business transactions**, or records of buying and selling goods, to historic events such as wars. The Mesopotamians carved cuneiform on clay tablets using a reed **stylus**.

Reading and Writing

Scribes were the masters of cuneiform reading and writing. They learned how to write cuneiform at scribe schools, called "tablet houses." Scribes also learned mathematics and other skills, and made math tables that helped people make calculations. They had to know how to record events, business dealings, and the daily activities of the king's court, government, and temples. Scribes also recorded the movement of the stars and planets. Mesopotamian people studied the movement of stars and planets to understand how the universe works.

Skilled Musicians

Music was an important part of ancient Mesopotamian cultures. Many cuneiform tablets show musical scenes or instructions for how to tune ancient instruments. In 1929, Leonard Woolley discovered three **lyres** and one harp in the royal cemetery of Ur. Lyres are also depicted on the Standard of Ur.

There were more than 500 different cuneiform signs.

History Up Close

Even after cuneiform replaced pictograms, symbols continued to be used on cylinder seals. These tiny carved stone cylinders were a form of personal signature. They were rolled across wet clay to mark personal letters and business documents. This cylinder seal from the 7th century B.C.E. is made from a type of rock. The impression on the cylinder shows two horses rearing up on their hind legs on both sides of a winged figure.

cylinder seal

impression

GODS, FAITH, AND MYTHOLOGY

Religion was central to everyday life in Mesopotamia. It influenced how people behaved and how they lived. Mesopotamians worshiped many gods and goddesses. They built grand temples to them and dedicated entire cities to them. People honored the gods and looked to them for protection from floods, disease, and enemy attacks.

Gods and Goddesses

Each civilization added its own gods to those already known. The city-states were dedicated to specific gods that protected them. These gods were known as patron gods. For example, the Sumerians worshiped Inanna, who was the patron goddess of the city of Uruk. Marduk was the patron god of Babylon. Priests and priestesses performed **rituals** in the temple at the top of ziggurats to make the gods and goddesses happy. Ea, An, and Enlil were three of the most powerful Mesopotamian gods. Ea was the creator and protector of human beings. An was the sky god, and Enlil determined human fate.

Fashioned from Clay

In one Mesopotamian myth, Enlil was said to have made humans out of clay and blood. Sumerian clay tablets tell of An killing another god and using his body and blood, mixed with clay, to create humans who would do the physical work for gods.

The Afterlife

Death was not considered the end for the ancient Mesopotamians. They believed their spirits lived on after their bodies died. The spirit went to a dark **netherworld** to find its place. The body had to be buried first, and the dead person's family had to give offerings of food and drink, or else the dead person's ghost would wander around and might haunt the living.

This sculpture depicts a lamassu, which is a protective god with a human head, bull's body, and wings. These figures were often placed at the entrances of homes and other buildings to protect the people who entered there.

History Up Close

The *Epic of Gilgamesh* was the first superhero story. It was written as an epic poem on 12 cuneiform tablets—3,000 lines of carefully handwritten cuneiform. The epic is also the oldest surviving work of literature. This tablet was found in modern Iraq, and dates to 2003–1595 B.C.E. Gilgamesh, the hero of the story, may have been based on a real Sumerian king. Gilgamesh travels, has adventures, slays monsters and demons, learns about a great flood, and descends to the underworld.

tablet

TRADE AND WAR

Mesopotamia's civilizations were long-lasting and powerful. For thousands of years, the different empires grew and expanded, taking over territory through war and settlement. Mesopotamia dominated trade and influenced culture. Its civilizations were well known to many other cultures, including the Egyptians, Nubians, Harappans, and Persians.

Trading Networks

Mesopotamians traded silver, wool, and grains for tin, copper, gold, wood, **lapis lazuli**, and pearls. After the invention of the wheel, carts and chariots allowed Mesopotamian traders to travel long distances for trade. Roads were built following the course of the Euphrates and Tigris rivers to the north and west. Other trade routes zigzagged through the Zagros Mountains in the area that is now northwest Iraq, Iran, and southeast Turkey. Traders and merchants also sailed the Persian Gulf to the Arabian Sea and Indus Valley.

This is a Persian soldier of around the 500s B.C.E., armed with a bow, spear, and shield. He is depicted on a wall in the ancient city of Babylon. The wall now survives in the collection of the Pergamon Museum in Berlin, Germany.

War

One way Mesopotamian empires expanded was through war. They conquered foreign territories and forced them to pay **tribute** to the Mesopotamian king each year. The tribute helped the king pay for his army, roads, and building projects. If the territories refused to pay, the Mesopotamian army invaded and took what the territory owed. No one wanted to go to war with the Mesopotamians, who were known to be very strong in war. Mesopotamian city-states fought with each other, as well. As the population grew, there were more wars fought over control of territory.

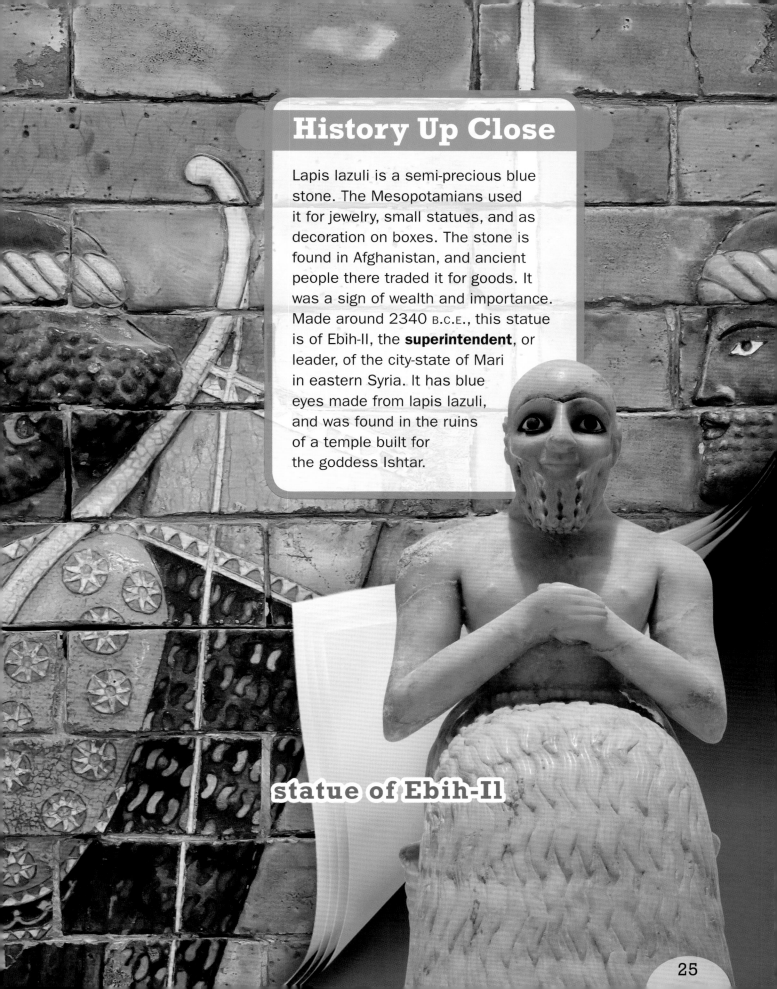

History Up Close

Lapis lazuli is a semi-precious blue stone. The Mesopotamians used it for jewelry, small statues, and as decoration on boxes. The stone is found in Afghanistan, and ancient people there traded it for goods. It was a sign of wealth and importance. Made around 2340 B.C.E., this statue is of Ebih-Il, the **superintendent**, or leader, of the city-state of Mari in eastern Syria. It has blue eyes made from lapis lazuli, and was found in the ruins of a temple built for the goddess Ishtar.

statue of Ebih-Il

PAST TO PRESENT

The civilizations of ancient Mesopotamia were often mentioned in the writings of **scholars**, travelers, and traders. However, the tells of Mesopotamia remained mostly untouched for thousands of years. It was only in the 1800s that excavations revealed the full extent of these culturally rich civilizations.

Visitors to the British Museum in London, England, get a close-up look at the museum's collection of cuneiform tablets, which is the largest in the world.

Digging Up History

People were fascinated by the discoveries made by early archaeologists. In 1857, a method of translating cuneiform into English was discovered. Thousands of tablets could finally be read and understood. Archaeological research changed with each Mesopotamian discovery. Archaeologists knew that simply finding artifacts was not enough. They needed to understand information about the site they were digging, such as how many civilizations might have lived there, and how the site had changed over time.

Rise and Fall

After thousands of years, which saw many innovations, empires, and cultures, invaders from Persia (modern-day Iran) conquered Mesopotamia. The new conquerors, and others that came after, brought new cultures and religions. They also built their cities on top of the ruins of old Mesopotamian city-states. Archaeologists dig through these ruins to find clues about life in the ancient world.

Archaeology Today

War and unrest in Iraq and Syria have made it unsafe to continue excavating this region. Many sites, such as Ur in Iraq, have been bombed. Others have been looted by treasure hunters and thieves who steal the ancient artifacts to sell them. **Extremist** religious groups have damaged Mari, Nimrud, and Nineveh. Libraries and museums in Mosul, Iraq, have been also looted.

History Up Close

The Nimrud Ivories are artifacts that show how large Mesopotamia's trade networks were. They are carved plaques and figures that date to the 9th and 7th centuries B.C.E. Uncovered by archaeologists in the ancient Assyrian city of Nimrud, the detailed carvings were at one time covered with gold and semi-precious stones and may have been set into pieces of furniture. Made in Egypt or other areas of what is now the Middle East, their presence in Mesopotamia illustrates how the ancient Mesopotamians traded with other cultures and civilizations.

Dig Deeper!

Many of the Nimrud Ivories are on display in museums in Britain and other parts of the world. Should these Mesopotamian treasures be kept in foreign museums, or sent back to Iraq? Are there reasons why they are safer in foreign museums?

27

MAKE A MODEL ZIGGURAT

Mud bricks were the main building material of Mesopotamia. The ancient Mesopotamians made mud bricks from the materials that were available: mud, straw, and pebbles. The mud mixture was poured into rectangular molds that were left to dry and harden in the sun. Once hardened, the bricks were used to build towering ziggurats and other structures.

Rebuilding the Ziggurat

The Ziggurat of Ur was first built around 2300 B.C.E. It has been rebuilt many times. The Iraqi government ordered its reconstruction in the 1900s. To rebuild the massive structure, archaeologists studied ancient carvings and texts written in cuneiform to figure out how the ziggurat was built thousands of years ago.

The Ziggurat of Ur was discovered and excavated in the 1920s and 1930s.

28

Activity:

Build a Ziggurat

Make a ziggurat and discover more about the ancient Mesopotamians.

Instructions

1. Cover your work surface with a layer of newspaper.
2. Break off a chunk of clay. Form it into a flattened rectangle. Ask an adult to help you cut straight edges with the modeling knife.
3. Make a smaller rectangle and place it on top of the first. Use your fingers to smooth together the seam between the two levels.
4. Add a third rectangle on top. Form a small square for the temple and place it at the top. Construct three staircases leading to the top of the ziggurat. Look at the labeled diagram for reference.
5. When the model is complete, place it on a baking sheet.
6. With adult supervision, bake the clay following the instructions on the modeling clay package.

The Challenge

Once your model is complete, take a closer look. Why do you think it may have been built with this design? Many Mesopotamian gods were believed to live in far-off mountains. How does the shape of a ziggurat support this idea?

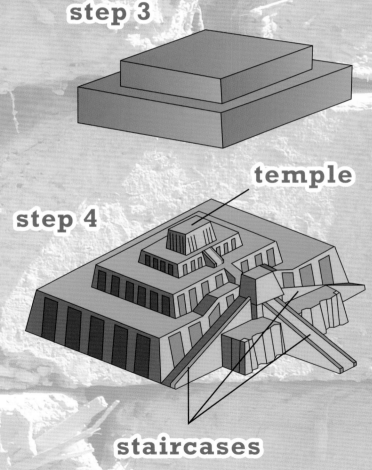

step 3

step 4

temple

staircases

GLOSSARY

Note: Some bold-faced words are defined where they appear in the text.

agricultural irrigation Water supplied to land to grow crops, often from rivers or streams via channels

analyze To examine

aqueducts Human-made channels for water

archaeologists People who study the past through the materials people left behind

ards Ancient agricultural tools that resemble hoes for making grooves in soil

artifacts Objects made by humans that give information about a culture or historical way of life

axles Shafts on or with which a wheel or pair of wheels turn

buttresses Supports built against a wall or building

city-states Cities, that with their surrounding territories, form independent states or kingdoms

coronation The ceremony of crowning a ruler, such as a king or queen

craftspeople People who practice a trade or a craft

cultures The customs, arts, behaviors, and institutions of a specific nation, people, or social group

empires Groups of different states or countries that are ruled by one authority or government

excavations Sites that have been dug out

extremist Having radical ideas that are often political or religious

fertile Able to grow plants or crops

habitation The process or evidence of people living in a particular place

historian An expert in the history of a time period, region, or significant event

impression An image created by stamping or pressing something on a material

innovations New methods, ideas, or inventions that create change and sometimes modernization

interpret To figure out

lagoons Bodies of salt water separated from the sea by a sandbank or reef

lapis lazuli A deep blue semi-precious stone mined in ancient Afghanistan that people in the ancient world prized for its beauty

lyres U-shaped string instruments

netherworld The underworld in the Mesopotamian religion, where the souls of people went when they died; It had many different names that mean earth of no return, darkness, or grave

onagers Wild animals from the horse family, similar to a donkey

prehistoric Describes a period of time before history was written down

rituals Religious ceremonies in which certain actions are performed in specific ways to satisfy gods or a ruler

scholars People who are highly educated and are experts in certain fields of study

scribes People who copy documents

silt Fine sand, clay, or other material carried by running water

sophisticated Something that is complex or highly developed

stela/stelae (pl.) Vertical stone slabs covered with inscriptions and images to commemorate a person or event

stylus A writing tool that has a pointed end for scratching letters or symbols (sometimes on wax tablets)

taxes Money paid to the government to pay for public facilities, such as roads

trade Buying and selling goods

tribute Valuable items or goods paid to the city-state, much like taxes are paid today

Learning More

Want to learn more about ancient Mesopotamia? Check out these resources.

Books

Gruber, Beth. *Ancient Iraq: Archaeology Unlocks the Secrets of Iraq's Past*. National Geographic Children's Books, 2007.

Nardo, Don. *Mesopotamia*. Capstone Press, 2013.

Roxburgh, Ellis. *The Mesopotamian Empires*. Cavendish Square, 2016.

Shuter, Jane. *Mesopotamia*. Heinemann, 2016.

Steele, Philip, and John Farndon. *Eyewitness Mesopotamia*. DK Books, 2007.

Wood, Alix. *Uncovering the Culture of Ancient Mesopotamia*. PowerKids Press, 2016.

Websites

This British Museum site lets viewers explore stories, investigate topics, and question their knowledge of Mesopotamian people and cultures.
www.mesopotamia.co.uk

The University of Pennsylvania Museum of Archaeology and Anthropology presents an overview on the peoples of ancient Mesopotamia.
www.penn.museum/sites/iraq/?page_id=16

Take a crash course in ancient Mesopotamia from PBS Learning.
http://bit.ly/2lDkj70

Learn more about the cradle of civilization at this site, which includes links to additional resources about ancient Mesopotamia.
www.ushistory.org/civ/4.asp

INDEX

ABOUT THE AUTHOR

Growing up, Ellen Rodger was fascinated with mummies, including King Tut, mummy horror movies, and the real Egyptian mummy exhibited in her small hometown museum. She has edited books on ancient civilizations, mythology, and explorers, and is the author of many books for children and adults.